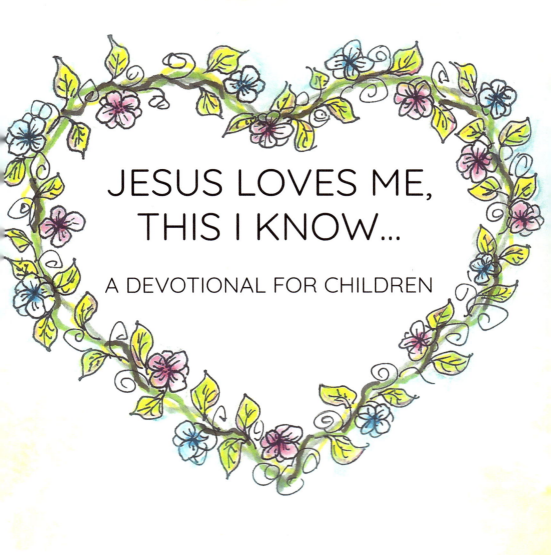

JESUS LOVES ME, THIS I KNOW...

A DEVOTIONAL FOR CHILDREN

By Michele Bard
Illustrated by Robert C. Brinser

Copyright ©2024 by Michele Bard
All rights reserved.

Softcover ISBN: 979-8-3481-1857-0
Hardcover ISBN: 979-8-348-1-2925-5
Printed in the United States of America

All Scripture quotations, unless otherwise indicated, are taken from the Holy Bible, New International Version®, NIV®. Copyright ©1973, 1978, 1984, 2011 by Biblica, Inc.™ Used by permission of Zondervan. All rights reserved worldwide. www.zondervan.com. The "NIV" and "New International Version" are trademarks registered in the United States Patent and Trademark Office by Biblica, Inc.™

To order more copies of this book, please visit:
JesusLovesMeBook.com

Dedication

This book was written to bring glory to God and to draw those who read it closer to Him. It is dedicated to the little lambs in my life: Abigail, Charlotte, Emma Grace, Jacob, Job, Kearsey, Kyren, Liam, and Natalia. Special thanks to my husband, George, for his support; my sister, Lori, for her insight and encouragement; Bob Brinser, for his beautiful artwork; and Scott Eash for helping to bring it all to fruition.

We are all sheep in need of the Good Shepherd, Jesus. Join Lovee Lamb, and her friends, on their journey to learn how much Jesus loves them!

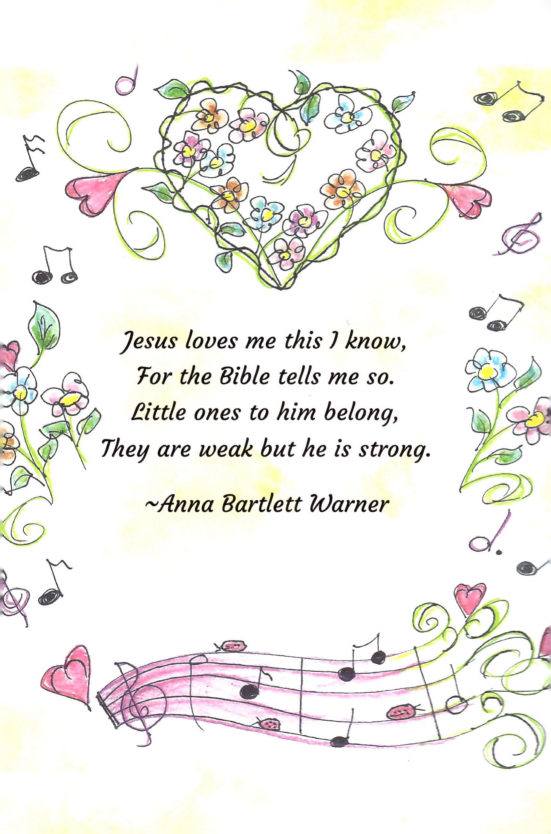

Jesus loves me, this I know because...

He created the world for me to live in and enjoy!

Genesis 1:31 – 2:1

God saw all that He had made and it was very good...Thus the heavens and the earth were completed in all their vast array.

Thoughts for discussion:

1. What are some things that God created?
2. What is your favorite animal, plant, or thing that God created? Why is this your favorite?
3. What are some ways that you can help take care of God's creation?

BIBLE TRUTH: Adam named all the animals! (Gen. 2:19)

PRAYER: Dear Jesus, Thank you for creating such a beautiful world for me. Please help me to take good care of it. Amen.

Jesus loves me, this I know because...

He made me!

Psalm 139: 13-14

For you created my inmost being, you knit me together in my mother's womb. I praise you because I am fearfully and wonderfully made; your works are wonderful, I know this full well.

Thoughts for discussion:

1. What are some ways God made you special?
2. How can you help others to see that God made them special too?

BIBLE TRUTH: God knows how many hairs are on your head! (Matt. 10:30)

PRAYER: Dear Jesus, Thank you for loving me and making me special! Help me to remember how much you love me. Amen.

He has a plan for my life.

Jeremiah 29:11

For I know the plans I have for you, declares the Lord, plans to prosper you and not to harm you, plans to give you hope and a future.

Thoughts for discussion:

1. What do you think God wants you to be when you grow up?
2. What are some ways you can share God's love in that job?

BIBLE TRUTH: God knows everything about us. (Psalm 119:168)

PRAYER: Dear Jesus, Thank you for loving me so much you have a plan for my life. Show me the way to You. Amen.

Jesus loves me, this I know because...

He came to earth to die for my sins so that I can live with Him forever.

John 3:16

For God so loved the world that he gave his one and only Son, that whoever believes in him shall not perish but have eternal life.

Thoughts for discussion:

1. Why did Jesus come to earth?
2. What do you think living forever with Jesus will be like?

BIBLE TRUTH: Believing in Jesus is the only way to live forever in Heaven. (John 3:36)

PRAYER: Dear Jesus, Thank you for loving me so much that you died for my sins. Help me to see my need for You and trust in You for the forgiveness of my sins. Amen.

Jesus loves me, this I know because...

He wants me to become more like Him.

Galatians 5:22

But the fruit of the Spirit is love, joy, peace, patience, kindness, goodness, faithfulness, gentleness and self-control. Against such things there is no law.

Thoughts for discussion:

1. Think about today. What is one way you showed a fruit of the Spirit to another person?
2. Which fruit of the Spirit is the easiest for you to demonstrate, which is the hardest?

BIBLE TRUTH: We should always strive to be more like God. (I Timothy 4:7-8)

PRAYER: Dear Jesus, Please help me to show the fruit of the Spirit to other people. Please give me your strength when it is hard. Amen.

Jesus loves me, this I know because...

He gives me rules to live by to keep me safe and happy, and help me be more like Him.

Exodus 20:3-17 (paraphrased)

Always put God first, do not worship anything other than God, do not misuse God's name, ... honor your father and mother, do not murder, ... do not steal, do not lie, do not wish for things that other people have.

Thoughts for discussion:

1. How can you put God first in your life?
2. Do you sometimes do things that God said not to do? When that happens, how do you feel? Are you willing to tell God you are sorry?
3. What would make it easier for you to obey God's rules?

BIBLE TRUTH: God wrote His rules on stone tablets. (Exodus 24:12)

PRAYER: Dear Jesus, Thank you for loving me so much that You gave me rules by which to live. Help me to follow your rules and stay close to You. Amen.

Jesus loves me, this I know because...

He wants me to obey and honor my parents.

Ephesians 6:1-3

Children, obey your parents in the Lord, for this is right. "Honor your father and mother" – which is the first commandment with a promise – "so that it may go well with you and that you may enjoy long life on the earth."

Thoughts for discussion:

1. What are some ways that you obeyed your parent(s) today?
2. What are some ways you can show honor to your parent(s)?

BIBLE TRUTH: When you obey your parents, Jesus is pleased! (Colossians 3:20)

PRAYER: Dear Jesus, Please help me to obey my mom and dad (or those who care for me) even when it is hard. Amen.

Jesus loves me, this I know because...

He wants me to love others, just like He loves me.

Galatians 5:14

For the entire law is fulfilled in keeping this one command: "Love your neighbor as yourself."

Thoughts for discussion:

1. How did you show God's love to someone else today?
2. Sometimes this is very hard. How can God help us to love someone with whom we do not get along?

BIBLE TRUTH: The Good Samaritan showed love to his enemy. (Luke 10:25-37)

PRAYER: Dear Jesus, Please help me to show your love to people around me, even people who do not like me. Give me the courage to follow your rules. Amen.

Jesus loves me, this I know because...

He gives me His strength.

Philipians 4:13

I can do all things through him who gives me strength.

Thoughts for discussion:

1. How did God give you strength today?
2. Did you use God's strength to help another person today? If so, how?

BIBLE TRUTH: God gives us His strength so that He will be praised when we use it to serve others. (I Peter 4:11)

PRAYER: Dear Jesus, Help me to lean on your strength, especially when I feel weak. Help me to let others know that it is your strength that makes me strong. Amen.

Jesus loves me, this I know because...

He died for my sins and rose again!

Romans 4:25

He was delivered over to death for our sins and was raised to life for our justification.

Thoughts for discussion:

1. What are some things that you did today that made Jesus sad?
2. Have you trusted in Jesus to forgive you of your sins?

BIBLE TRUTH: Because Jesus was raised from the dead, we can trust God to raise us up too! (Romans 8:11)

PRAYER: Dear Jesus, Please forgive me for the things I did today that made you sad. Thank you for dying for my sins. Help me to trust in You as my Savior. Amen.

Jesus loves me, this I know because...

He cares for me.

Mark 10:16

And he took the children in his arms, placed his hands on them and blessed them.

I Peter 5:7

Cast all your anxiety on him because he cares for you.

Thoughts for discussion:

1. What are some ways God cares for you?
2. What are some worries you have that you need to give to God?

BIBLE TRUTH: Jesus gives us peace that others cannot understand. (Philippians 4:7)

PRAYER: Dear Jesus, Thank you for taking care of me. Help me to always trust you. Amen.

He wants me to live with Him forever.

John 14:3

And if I go and prepare a place for you, I will come back and take you to be with me that you also may be where I am.

Thoughts for discussion:

1. What do you think Heaven will be like?
2. What are some ways that you want to show Jesus how much you love Him when you get there (singing, dancing, praying, etc)?

BIBLE TRUTH: There are thousands and thousands of angels singing in Heaven! (Revelation 5:11-12)

PRAYER: Dear Jesus, Thank you for making Heaven a beautiful place for me to live with You someday. Amen.

Jesus loves me, this I know because...

He prays for me.

Hebrews 7:25

Therefore, he is able to save completely those who come to God through him, because he always lives to intercede for them.

Thoughts for discussion:

1. What cares or concerns did you share with Jesus today?
2. How does it make you feel that Jesus listens to your prayers and cares about your day?

BIBLE TRUTH: You can talk to Jesus anytime because He is never asleep. (Psalm 121)

PRAYER: Dear Jesus, Thank you for always hearing my prayers and caring for me. Help me to remember that I can always talk to You. Amen.

www.ingramcontent.com/pod-product-compliance
Lightning Source LLC
Chambersburg PA
CBHW062046310125
21208CB00013B/244